GIFTED & TALENTED

To develop your child's gifts and talents

MATH

GIFTED & TALENTED

To develop your child's gifts and talents

MATH

A Workbook for Ages 6–8

Written by Nancy Casolaro
Edited by Susan Amerikaner and Ann Laner
Illustrated by Leesa Whitten
Designed by Zofia H. Kostyrko

Lowell House
Juvenile
Los Angeles

Contemporary Books
Chicago

Manufactured in the United States of America

ISBN 1-56565-039-5

10 9 8 7 6

Cover design: Brenda Leach
Cover illustration: Kerry Manwaring

GIFTED AND TALENTED WORKBOOKS will help develop your child's natural talents and gifts by providing activities to enhance critical and creative thinking skills. These skills of logic and reasoning teach children **how** to think. They are precisely the skills emphasized by teachers of gifted and talented children.

Thinking skills are the skills needed to be able to learn anything at any time. Unlike events, words, and teaching methods, thinking skills never change. If a child has a grasp of how to think, school success and even success in life will become more assured. In addition, the child will become self-confident as he or she approaches new tasks with the ability to think them through and discover solutions.

GIFTED AND TALENTED WORKBOOKS present these skills in a unique way, combining the basic subject areas of reading, language arts, and math with thinking skills. The top of each page is labeled to indicate the specific thinking skill developed. Here are some of the skills you will find:

- Deduction – the ability to reach a logical conclusion by interpreting clues

- Understanding relationships – the ability to recognize how objects, shapes, and words are similar or dissimilar; to classify and categorize

- Sequencing – the ability to organize events, numbers; to recognize patterns

- Inference – the ability to reach logical conclusions from given or assumed evidence

- Creative thinking – the ability to generate unique ideas; to compare and contrast the same elements in different situations; to present imaginative solutions to problems

How to Use Gifted & Talented Workbooks

Each book contains activities that challenge children. The activities vary in range from easier to more difficult. You may need to work with your child on many of the pages, especially with the child who is a non-reader. However, even a non-reader can master thinking skills, and the sooner your child learns how to think, the better. Read the directions to your child, and if necessary, explain them. Let your child choose to do the activities that interest him or her. When interest wanes, stop. A page or two at a time may be enough, as the child should have fun while learning.

It is important to remember that these activities are designed to teach your child **how to think,** not how to find the right answer. Teachers of gifted children are never surprised when a child discovers a new "right" answer. For example, a child may be asked to choose the object that doesn't belong in this group: a table, a chair, a book, a desk. The best answer is **book,** since all the others are furniture. But a child could respond that all of them belong because they all could be found in an office. The best way to react to this type of response is to praise the child and gently point out that there is another answer too. While creativity should be encouraged, your child must look for the best and most **suitable** answer.

GIFTED AND TALENTED WORKBOOKS have been written and designed by teachers. Educationally sound and endorsed by leaders in the gifted field, this series will benefit any child who demonstrates curiosity, imagination, a sense of fun and wonder about the world, and a desire to learn. These books will open your child's mind to new experiences and help fulfill his or her true potential.

Sassy Hen lost her eggs. Her eggs are marked with numbers that are:

more than 5
less than 12

Circle the eggs that belong to Sassy.

Catch the king's butterflies. His butterflies are marked with numbers that are:

even numbers
less than 14

Circle the butterflies that belong to the king.

Geraldo Giraffe eats leaves with numbers that are:

odd numbers
more than 9

Circle the leaves that Geraldo will eat.

Can you find food for the Sneekle? Sneekles eat numbers that are:

> even numbers
> more than 8
> less than 20

Circle the things that the Sneekle will eat.

Can you find the Meecher's footprints? A Meecher's footprint is a number that is:

an odd number
more than 70
less than 100

Circle the Meecher's footprints.

93

99

87

75

63

74

81

86

101

72

98

79

Can you find the hats for this Blicking? A Blicking is a monster who only wears hats with numbers that are:

divisible by 3
less than 36
even numbers

Make a number puzzle for a friend.

Can you find the Numberoos? Numberoos have numbers that are:

Color this design, but use only **three** colors — and make sure that no shapes of the same color touch each other. Think before you color!

Color this design, but use only **four** colors — and make sure that no shapes of the same color touch each other. (It's a good idea to start by coloring the shapes that touch a lot of others.)

One of the numbers fell into the math contraption. Which one was it? Write the number on the empty ball.

Which number fell into the math contraption? Write the number on the empty circle.

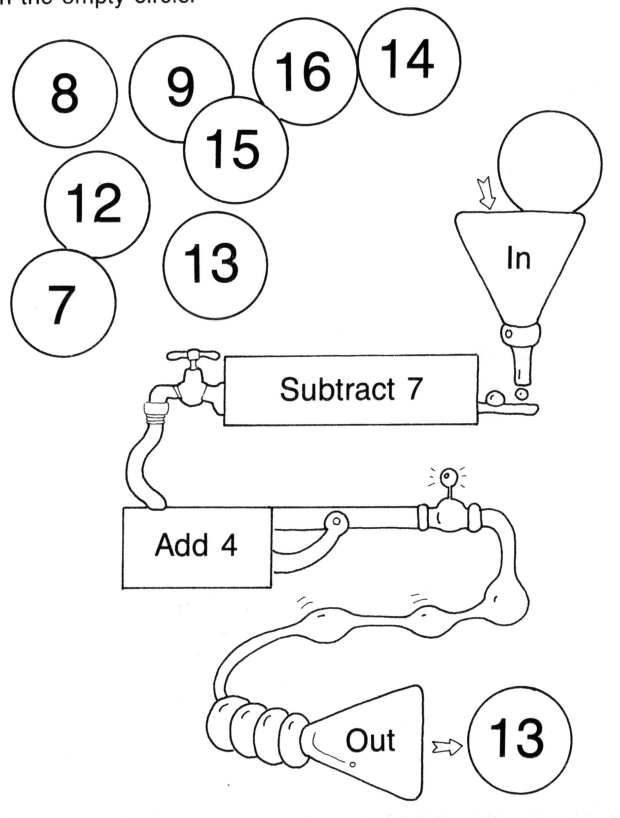

Which two numbers fell into the math contraption? Write the numbers on the empty circles.

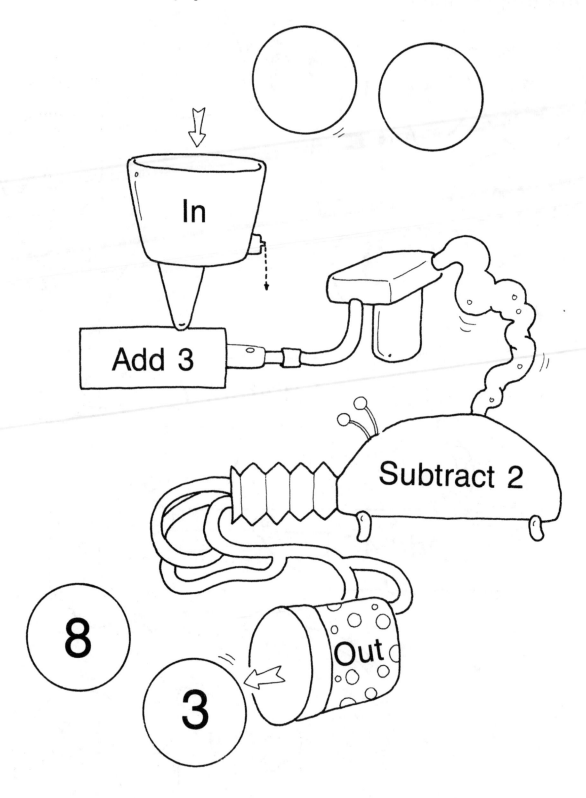

Which numbers fell into the math contraption? Write the numbers on the empty circles.

Make your own math contraption, and get a friend to try to solve it.

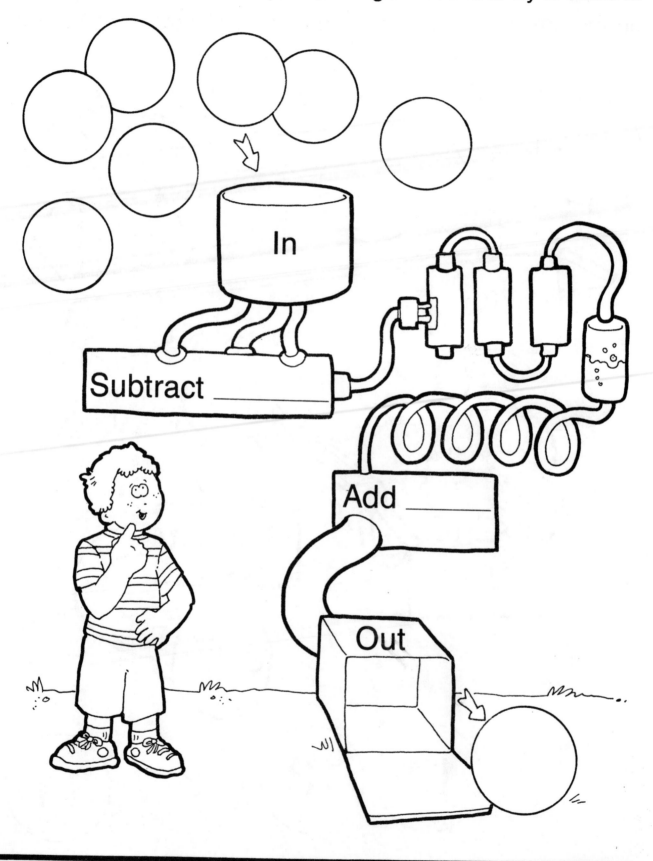

Redwood School held an apple-eating contest. Read all the clues. Then write the correct names next to the number of apples he or she ate.

Name	Apples
A._____	16
B._____	12
C._____	10
D._____	6
E._____	4

1. Jamal ate the most apples.
2. Matt ate 10 less than Jamal.
3. Rachel did not eat more than Matt.
4. Eli ate more than Matt, but less than Sarah.

Michele, Kevin, Daniel, and Amanda played Space Pirates. Read all the clues and write the correct name next to each score.

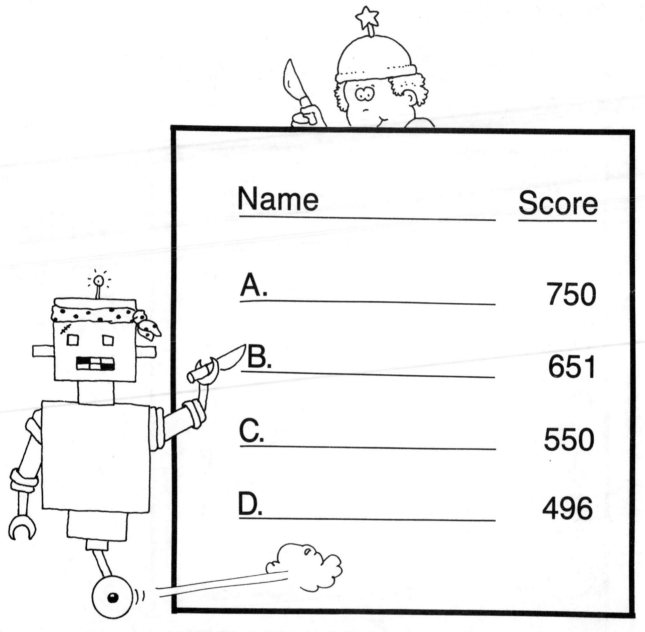

Name	Score
A.	750
B.	651
C.	550
D.	496

1. If Kevin had scored 100 more points, he would have had the highest score.
2. Amanda scored the highest.
3. Michele scored 200 points less than Amanda.
4. What was Daniel's score?

Megan, Tyrone, Brittany, and Teddy have their birthdays in November. Read all the clues. Then write each name next to the correct date.

Name	Date
A.	November 4
B.	November 11
C.	November 15
D.	November 20

1. Megan's birthday is one week after Teddy's.
2. Teddy's birthday comes first.
3. 7 + 8 equals Brittany's birthdate.
4. When is Tyrone's birthday?

Tara, Michael, Timmy, Nicky, and Soraya have marble collections. Read all the clues and write each name next to the correct number of marbles.

Name	Marbles
A. _____	20
B. _____	12
C. _____	8
D. _____	7
E. _____	5

1. Nicky has only green and blue marbles.
   He has 3 green marbles and 2 blue ones.
2. Soraya has 3 more marbles than Nicky.
3. Timmy has the most marbles.
4. Michael and Soraya together have the same number of marbles as Timmy.
5. How big is Tara's collection?

Courtney, Josh, Sean, Erin, and Damon have piggy banks. Read all the clues. Then write each name next to the correct amount in the piggy bank.

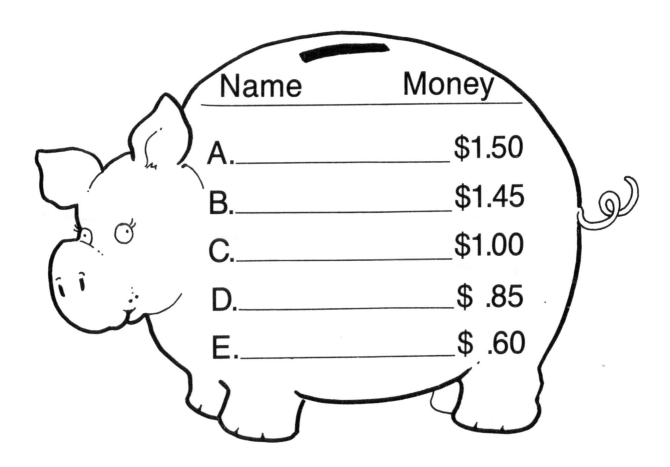

Name	Money
A.	$1.50
B.	$1.45
C.	$1.00
D.	$ .85
E.	$ .60

1. Courtney has 3 quarters and 1 dime.
2. Sean has 25 cents less than Courtney.
3. Erin has 6 quarters.
4. Sean and Courtney together have the same amount as Damon.
5. How much money is in Josh's bank?

The Hawks and the Eagles play soccer. Each player wears a different number on his or her shirt. The numbers are listed in the box. Read all the clues. Then write the correct number on each shirt.

4	7	9	11	12	19

The Hawks

The Eagles

1. All the Hawks wear numbers less than 10.
2. The tallest Eagle has the lowest number on his team.
3. The girls are wearing the even numbers.
4. The tallest Hawk does not have the highest number on his team.

Write the numbers 3, 4, 5, 6, 7, and 8 on the acrobats so that the sum of:

the top row is 4
the middle row is 12
the bottom row is 17

You can only use each number **one** time!

Write the numbers 3, 4, 5, 6, 7, and 8 on the balls so that the sum of:

the top row is 4
the middle row is 14
the bottom row is 15

You can only use each number **one** time!

Nicki's phone number begins with the numbers 5, 3, and 7 — but Nicki forgot what order the numbers are in. Arrange the numbers 5, 3, and 7 in as many different ways as you can. Write your combinations in the spaces below.

_____

_____

_____

_____

_____

Jessica forgot her score on the Space Man video game. She does remember that the numbers 1, 6, and 8 were in it. Write all the possible scores that Jessica could have had.

SCORE:

Jessica _____?_____

_____

_____

_____

_____

_____

_____

What is the lowest score Jessica could have had?_____

Which score could have been her highest?_____

A whistle in a vending machine costs 15¢. The machine only takes dimes, nickels, and pennies. Fill in the chart below with all the different combinations of coins that you could use to buy the 15¢ whistle. The first two are done for you.

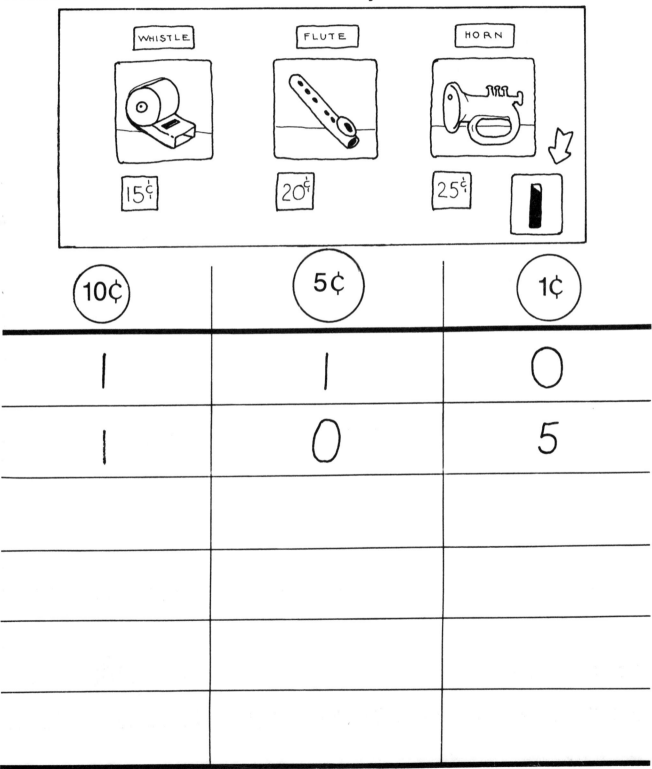

10¢	5¢	1¢
1	1	0
1	0	5

A toy robot in a vending machine costs 50¢. The machine only takes quarters, nickels, and dimes. Fill in the chart with all the different combinations of coins that you could use to buy a robot.

25¢	10¢	5¢

BEAR
5¢

CAR
10¢

ROBOT
50¢

Heather's piggy bank had only nickels and quarters in it. There were 2 less nickels than quarters. The total amount in the bank was $2.60.

Fill in the chart with combinations of nickels and quarters until you find the one that adds up to $2.60.

Hint: There are less than 50¢ worth of nickels in the bank!

25¢	5¢	Total

How many quarters were in the bank? _____

How many nickels were in it? _____

Read these clues:

Breanna is 2 years older than Ryan.
Alisha is 4 years older than Ryan.
If you add up all their ages, the total is 15.
Ryan is less than 6 years old.

Use the chart below to help you figure out the ages of Breanna, Ryan, and Alisha. Start by making a good **guess** about Ryan. Keep making guesses and filling in the chart — until you get the right combination.

Ryan	Breanna	Alisha	Total
Make a guess.	Add 2 to Ryan.	Add 4 to Ryan.	Is it 15?

34

Read all the clues:

Henry is 4 years older than Luis.
Jimmy is 5 years older than Luis.
If you add up all their ages, the total is 24.
Luis is less than 8 years old.

How old is Luis? _____ Henry? _____ Jimmy? _____

Luis	Henry	Jimmy	Total
Guess	Add 4 to Luis.	Add 5 to Luis.	Is it 24?

35

Read all the clues. Then use the chart to figure out the answers.

Hilary has read 2 more mystery books than Erica.
Morgan has read 5 more mystery books than Hilary.
If you add up all the mystery books they have read, the total is 18.

How many mystery books has Erica read? _____
Hilary? _____   Morgan? _____

Erica	Hilary	Morgan	Total
Guess	Add 2	Add _____	

Read all the clues. Then use the chart to figure out the correct answers.

Josh has 8 less Halloween candies than Adam.
Teddy has 6 less candies than Adam.
Adam has more than 10 candies.
If you add up their candies, the total is 31.

Adam	Josh	Teddy	Total

How many does Adam have? _____
Josh? _____   Teddy? _____

Make your own math puzzle. See if a friend can figure it out.

_____ ate _____ more apples than _____ .
_____ ate _____ more apples than _____ .

If you add up the apples they ate, the total is _____ .

Use the chart to help you.

Guess	Add _____	Add _____	Total

How many apples did _____ eat? _____
_____ ? _____   _____ ? _____

Think carefully (and use scrap paper if you need it) to answer the questions about the Art Attic.

Art Attic Prices
Watercolors . . . . 7¢
Markers . . . . 3¢
Crayons . . . . 2¢
Paper . . . . 5¢

1. Janna bought 2 items and spent 9¢. What items did she buy?

   _____

   _____

2. Carrie bought 2 items for 5¢. What items did she buy?

   _____

   _____

3. Jeremy bought 3 items and spent 10¢. Which items did he buy?

   _____

   _____

Think carefully and answer the questions about the Merry Mart.

Merry Mart Prices
Board Games....$5.00
Stuffed Toys.....$6.00
Books $4.00
Puzzles $3.00

1. Alison bought 2 different items and spent $8.00. Which items did she buy?

_____

_____

2. Brett spent $10.00 for 2 of the **same** items. What did he buy?

_____

_____

3. Jamie bought 2 gifts for his brother. He spent $9.00. What did he buy? (Hint: His brother doesn't like puzzles.)

_____

_____

Read carefully before you answer the questions.

Fast Food Place Prices
Hot dog . . . . $ .50
Hamburger . . . . . . $ .75
Milk . . . . $ .25
French fries . . . . . $ .50
Apples $1.00

1. Drew bought 3 different items for lunch and spent $1.50.
   What did he buy? (Hint: He doesn't like hot dogs.)

   _____

2. Cheryl spent $1.50 on 2 different items. What did she buy?
   (Hint: Cheryl doesn't like french fries.) _____

   _____   _____

3. Dara spent $1.25 for 3 items. (She doesn't like french fries,
   either.) What did she buy? _____

   _____

4. Chris spent $2.00 at Fast Food Place. He bought 4 different items. What did he buy?_____

_____

5. Erica wants a hamburger, a piece of fruit, and a drink. How much money does she need?_____

6. Heather had 4 items from the menu and spent $2.25. What did she have? (Hint: She doesn't eat apples or hot dogs.)

_____   _____

_____   _____

7. Matt bought 2 hamburgers, an order of french fries, and an apple. The cashier gave him $7.00 change. What bill did Matt give the cashier?_____

8. If you had $2.00 for lunch at Fast Food Place, what would you buy? _____

_____

Make up some tough questions of your own. Find a friend to figure out the answers.

Item	Prices

1. _____ bought 2 items and spent _____ .
   What did _____ buy?

2. _____ spent _____ on 3 different items.
   What did _____ buy?

3. _____ bought a _____ and a _____ .
   The cashier gave (him or her) _____ change.
   What did _____ give the cashier?

Jenny shot 3 arrows in archery class. Each arrow hit the target. Her total score was 10. What targets did she hit?

She could have hit _____ , _____ , and _____ .
She might have hit _____ , _____ , and _____ .
She may have hit _____ , _____ , and _____ .

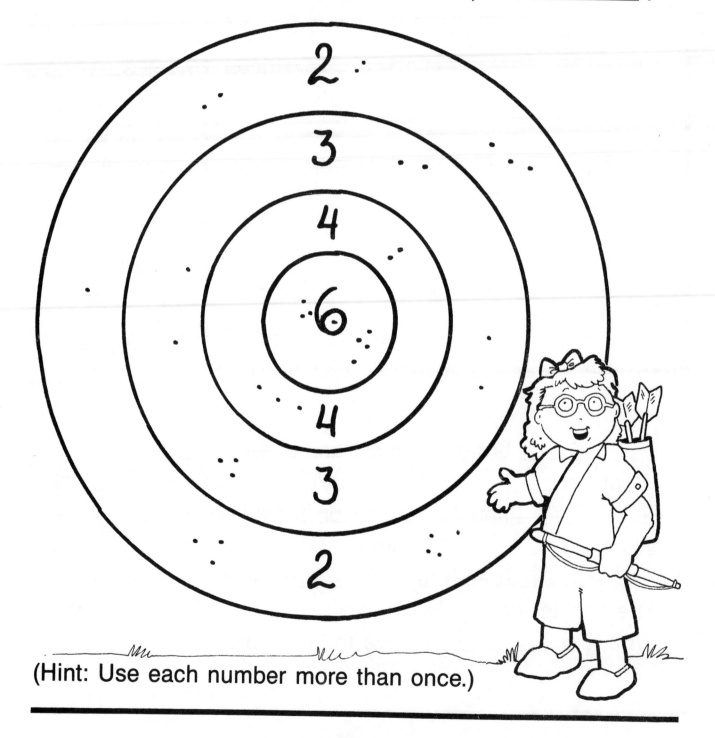

(Hint: Use each number more than once.)

Eric zapped 3 space ships on the video game. His total score was 15. Circle the space ships he zapped.

Can you solve this puzzle? It isn't easy!
Here are the clues:

The sum of each side must equal 12.
You can only use whole numbers less than 9.
A number can't be used more than **once** on each side.

It's a good idea to start by listing all the combinations of 3 numbers that can add up to 12, such as 8 + 3 + 1 and 4 + 2 + 6.

Think how the first two numbers in each box relate to each other. Which number will make the **last** two numbers relate to each other in the same way? Circle that number and write it on the line. The first one is done for you.

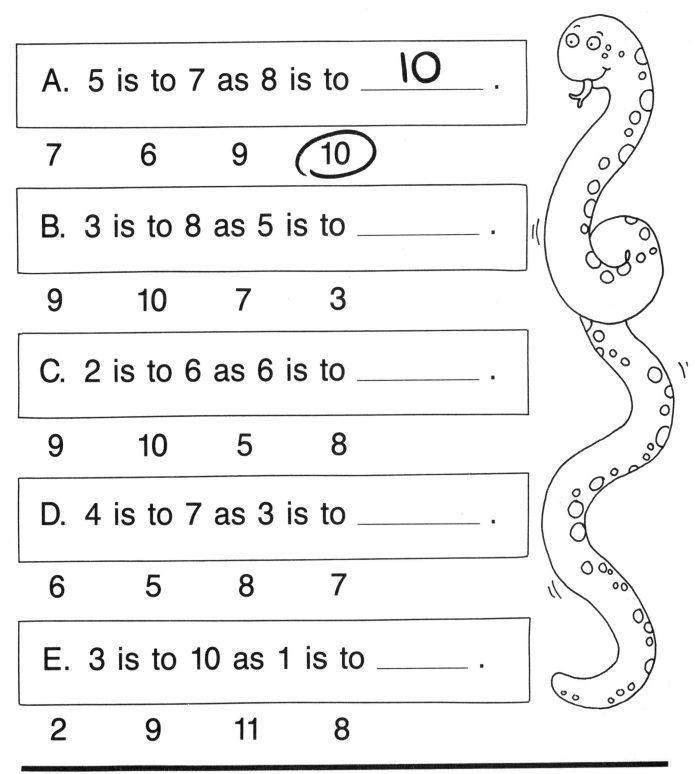

A. 5 is to 7 as 8 is to __10__ .

7   6   9   (10)

B. 3 is to 8 as 5 is to _____ .

9   10   7   3

C. 2 is to 6 as 6 is to _____ .

9   10   5   8

D. 4 is to 7 as 3 is to _____ .

6   5   8   7

E. 3 is to 10 as 1 is to _____ .

2   9   11   8

Which number will make the last two numbers relate in the same way as the first two? Circle the number and write it on the line.

A. 10 is to 7 as 6 is to _____ .

10   7   3   9

B. 12 is to 7 as 15 is to _____ .

5   20   19   10

C. 8 is to 14 as 6 is to _____ .

12   0   15   17

D. 9 is to 13 as 8 is to _____ .

4   15   13   12

E. 17 is to 9 as 16 is to _____ .

7   10   6   8

See if your friends can finish your number sentences. You fill in the first two blanks with two numbers that relate in a special way. Have a friend fill in the blanks with two more numbers that relate in the same way.

A. | _____ is to _____ as _____ is to _____ . |

B. | _____ is to _____ as _____ is to _____ . |

C. | _____ is to _____ as _____ is to _____ . |

D. | _____ is to _____ as _____ is to _____ . |

E. | _____ is to _____ as _____ is to _____ . |

F. | _____ is to _____ as _____ is to _____ . |

Help the chef. Write each number below on the correct pizza.

Help the monster finish the sign. Write each number in the correct circle.

Help the robot fix the computer. Write each number in the correct circle.

Now make up your own puzzle for a friend.

Count the squares in the picture below.

How many squares do you see?

_____

Did you see
4 of these?

But that's not all! Look again. The smaller squares are
inside another square!

There are 5 squares in the picture.

Count all the squares in the picture below. Remember: some squares are **inside** other squares.

Hint: There are more than 10 squares.

How many squares did you find?

_____

Count the squares in the picture below. Remember to look for squares inside of other squares!

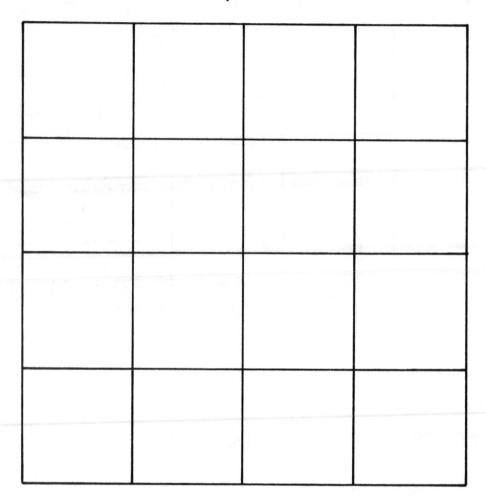

How many squares did you find? _____

Count the triangles in the picture. Don't forget: some triangles are inside other triangles!

How many triangles did you find? _____

Count the rectangles in the picture. Hint: a square is also a rectangle.

How many rectangles did you find? _____

Fill in the schedule below so that you can see all the shows at the neighborhood circus **before** lunch. One has been filled in for you.

Shows start at:

Mike's Magic Show
(45 minutes)

 10:30 A.M.    1:00 P.M.

Carlos the Clown
(30 minutes)

 10:00 A.M.    12:30 P.M.

Denise and Her Dancing Dogs
(30 minutes)

 10:15 A.M.    11:30 A.M.

SCHEDULE	
SHOW	TIME
1. _____	_____
2. Magic Show	10:30 A.M.
3. _____	_____
4. Lunch	12:00 P.M.

Fill in the schedule below so that you can see all the zoo shows in one day. One has been done for you. And don't forget lunch!

Bird Show (30 minutes)

Seal Show (30 minutes)

Elephant Show (45 minutes)

Monkey Show (45 minutes)

Shows start at:

1:30 P.M.   2:30 P.M.

10:30 A.M.   1:30 P.M.

11:00 A.M.   2:00 P.M.

12:30 P.M.   1:30 P.M.

SCHEDULE	
SHOW	TIME
1. Seal Show	10:30 A.M.
2.	
3. Lunch	12:00 - 1:00 P.M.
4.	
5.	

At the Fairy Tale Festival, shows are performed outdoors.
Plan your day so that you can see all the shows.

Shows start at:

Beauty and the Beast
(1 hour)

10:30 A.M.   11:30 A.M.

Jack and the Beanstalk
(1 hour)

10:00 A.M.   11:00 A.M.

Hansel and Gretel
(30 minutes)

10:00 A.M.   11:00 A.M.

Red Riding Hood
(1 hour)

12:00 P.M.   2:00 P.M.

ACT 1.

SCHEDULE	
SHOW	TIME
1. _____	_____
2. Hansel/Gretel	11:00 A.M.
3. _____	_____
4. Lunch	12:30 - 1:30 P.M.
5. _____	_____

Break the number code. Use the numbers 0, 2, and 4.
Each letter stands for one of these numbers. One has been
done for you. Figure out the rest.

CODE

A = ☐

B = ☐

C = 2

Figure out this code. Use the numbers 1, 2, 3, 4, and 5. One letter stands for each number. One has been done for you.

D	2		B			D	
+ A	3		− C			+ C	
B	5		E			A	

	E				C	
	− D				+ C	
	D				D	

Write the correct numbers in the code box.

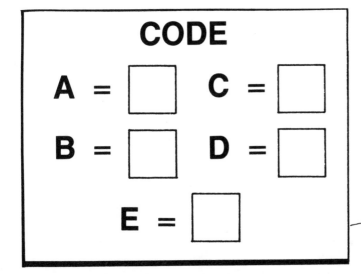

CODE

A = ☐   C = ☐

B = ☐   D = ☐

E = ☐

Solve the code. Use the numbers 2, 4, 5, 6, and 10. Fill in the code box with the correct numbers.

$$\begin{array}{r} A\ \square \\ +\ C\ \square \\ \hline E\ \square \end{array} \qquad \begin{array}{r} B\ \square \\ -\ D\ \square \\ \hline D\ \square \end{array} \qquad \begin{array}{r} E\ \square \\ +\ A\ \square \\ \hline B\ \square \end{array}$$

$$\begin{array}{r} B\ \square \\ -\ E\ \square \\ \hline A\ \square \end{array}$$

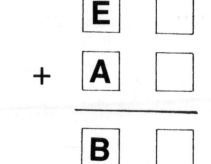

$$\boxed{E} + \boxed{E} \ = \ \boxed{B} + \boxed{C}$$

$$\square + \square \ = \ \square + \square$$

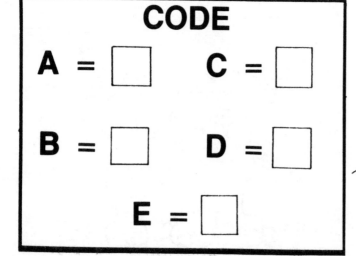

CODE

A = □   C = □

B = □   D = □

E = □

Solve this puzzle. Here are the rules:

1. The sum of each line must equal 10.

2. You can only use the numbers 1, 2, 3, 4, or 5.

3. You can only use each number once.

See how many solutions you can find to this puzzle. Here are the rules:

1. The sum of each line must equal 10.

2. You can only use the numbers 1, 2, 3, 4, 5, 6, or 7.

3. A number can be used only once in each solution.

There are many different answers. How many did you find?

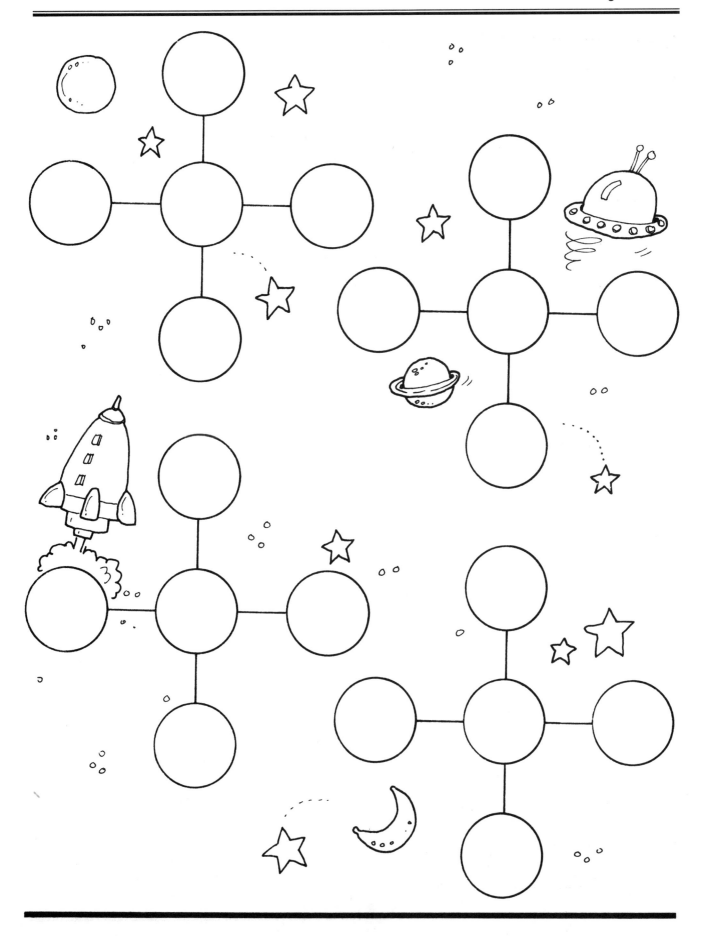

Here are the rules for this puzzle:

1. The sum of each line must equal 12.

2. You may only use the numbers 1, 2, 3, 4, 5, 6, 7, and 8.

3. A number can only be used once.

Hint: Start by listing all the combinations of 3 numbers that can make 12.

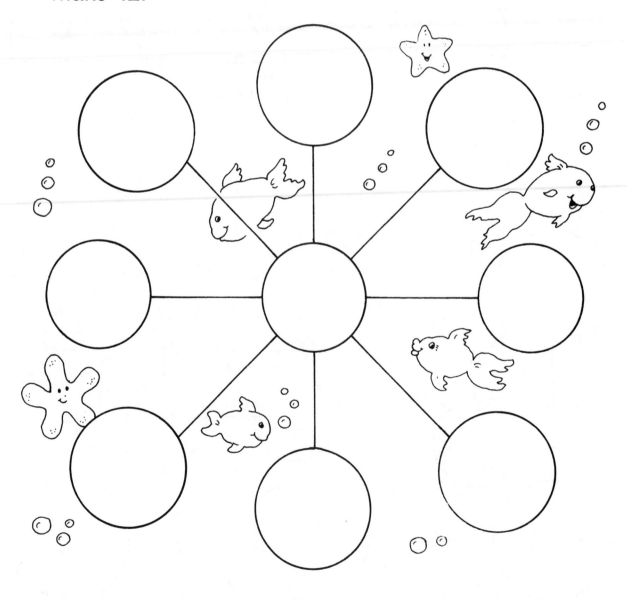

Try this puzzle. Here are the rules:

1. The sum of each side must equal 15.

2. You may only use the numbers 1, 2, 3, 4, 5, 6, 7, and 8.

3. A number can only be used once.

Hint: Think of all the combinations of 3 numbers that can make 15.

Make a puzzle for a friend. Be careful! Make sure you know the answer!

Can you solve this puzzle? Here are the rules:

1. The sum of each line must equal _____ .

2. You can only use numbers _____ .

3. You can only use a number once.

This machine is called COMBO. It combines the qualities of each set of objects to make a new set. For example, if we put in TRIANGLES and THINGS THAT ARE BLUE, we will end up with BLUE TRIANGLES!

List the objects that will come out of COMBO when we put in the two sets below. One has been done for you. Use extra paper if you need it!

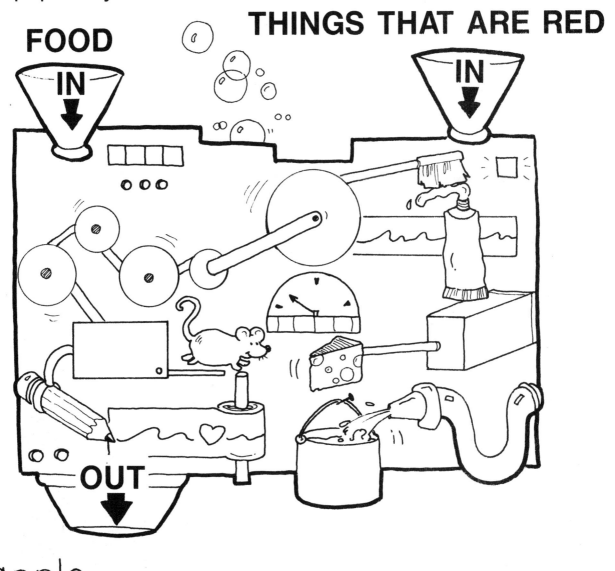

FOOD

THINGS THAT ARE RED

IN

IN

OUT

apple _____   _____   _____

_____   _____   _____

List the things that will come out of COMBO.

THINGS THAT HAVE WHEELS

THINGS YOU RIDE ON

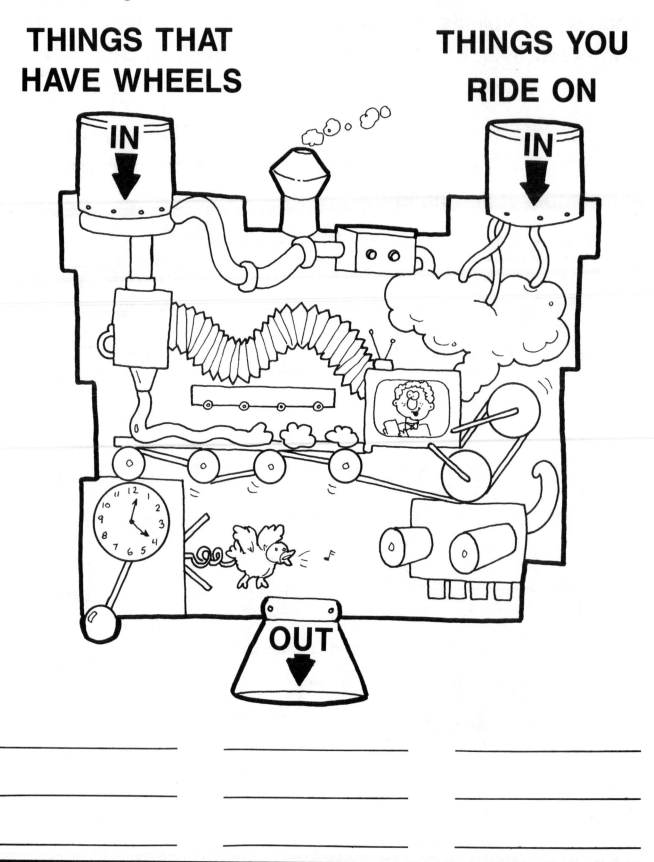

_____ _____ _____

_____ _____ _____

_____ _____ _____

List the numbers that will come out of COMBO.

WHOLE NUMBERS LESS THAN 20 AND GREATER THAN 0

ODD NUMBERS

List the numbers that will come out of COMBO.

EVEN NUMBERS

WHOLE NUMBERS
BETWEEN 40 AND 50

_____

Make this page for a friend.

This machine is called COMBO. It combines the sets of objects going in to form a new set of objects. List the things that will come out of COMBO.

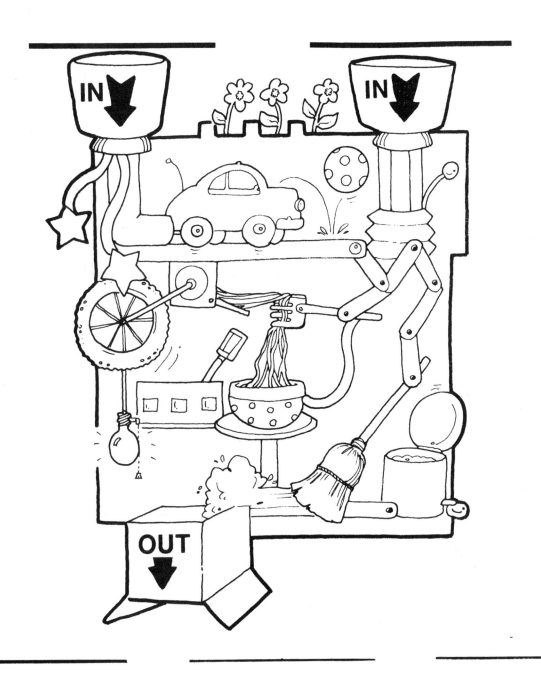

_____ _____ _____

_____ _____ _____

_____

Valerie, Stephen, Hilary, and Casey are having pizza. Where is each one sitting? Read all the clues below. Then write each name on the correct line.

Clues:

1. Stephen is sitting to the right of Hilary.

2. Valerie is sitting to the right of Casey.

3. Casey is wearing a baseball hat.

Keith, Sean, Courtney, and Max are eating dinner. Where is each one sitting? Read all the clues below. Then write each name on the correct line.

Clues:

1. Keith, Sean, and Courtney are eating spaghetti.

2. Sean is sitting to the left of Courtney.

3. Courtney is opposite someone eating a hamburger.

4. Max doesn't like spaghetti.

Matthew lives in West End. He went to see his grandmother in East End. He drove 8 miles to get there and stopped in one city along the way. Where did he stop?

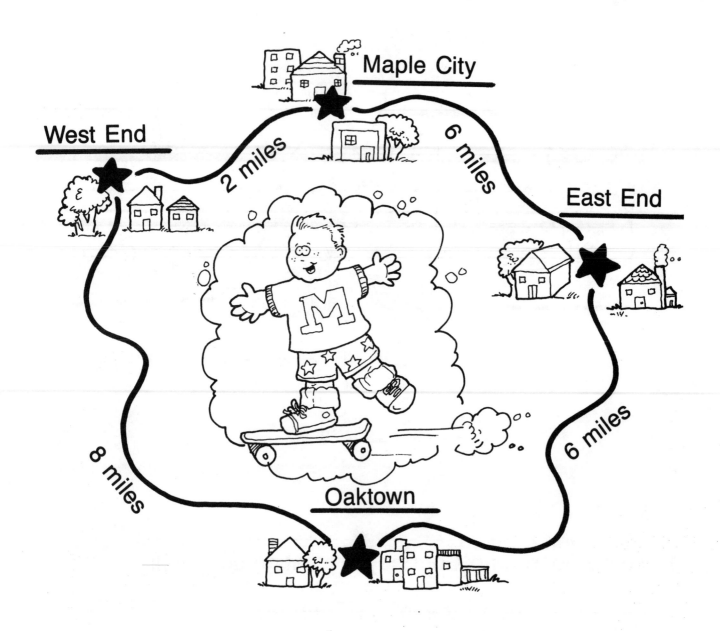

Matthew stopped in _____ .

Andrea lives in Oak Grove. She went to visit her friend in Elm City. She took the shortest route and stopped in 2 cities. Where did she stop?

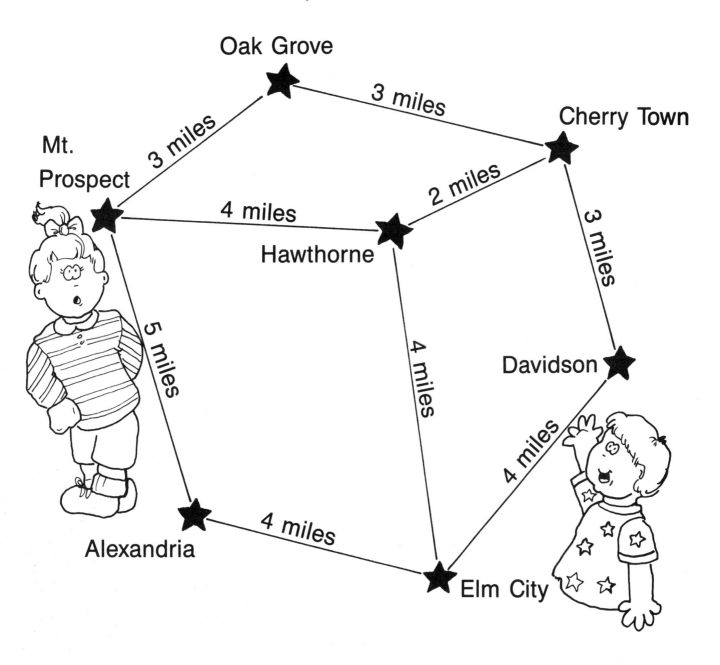

Andrea stopped in _____ and _____.

Niliphants come from the star Protozo. On Protozo money looks like this:

Loonies are worth 3¢.

Roonies are worth 6¢.

Zoonies are worth 9¢.

How much money is in each box?

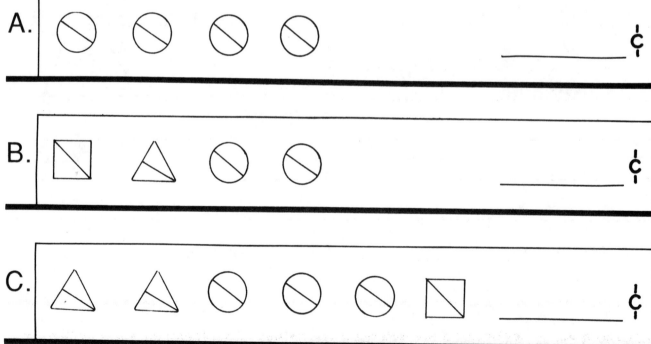

A. _____ ¢

B. _____ ¢

C. _____ ¢

A space vehicle on Protozo costs 18¢. List all the possible combinations of coins that a Niliphant could use to pay for the space vehicle. Two are done for you. Fill in the rest of the chart.

Zoonies	Roonies	Loonies
2	0	0
1	1	1

Pinkums come from another galaxy. Their money system is different from ours. Their system looks like this:

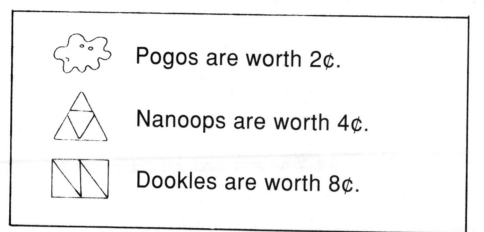

Pogos are worth 2¢.

Nanoops are worth 4¢.

Dookles are worth 8¢.

Write the answers to these questions:

A. How many Nanoops make one Dookle? _____

B. How many Pogos make one Dookle? _____

C. How many Pogos make one Nanoop? _____

A Pinkum has 20 cents. What are all the possible combinations of coins the Pinkum could have? Write the combinations in the chart below.

Dookles	Nanoops	Pogos

Heather ordered a pizza to feed 7 people. Draw lines to show how she should cut the pizza using only 3 straight lines.

Hint: The pieces do **not** have to be the same size.

Super Hint: All the lines do **not** have to go through the center!

Draw lines to show how to cut these cakes — following these rules:

1. There must be 8 pieces on each cake.

2. Each piece must be the same size.

3. You must use straight lines.

4. You must cut each cake in a different way.

Hint: There are 3 possible ways to cut the cakes.

Look in the box to find the shape that comes next. Circle the shape.

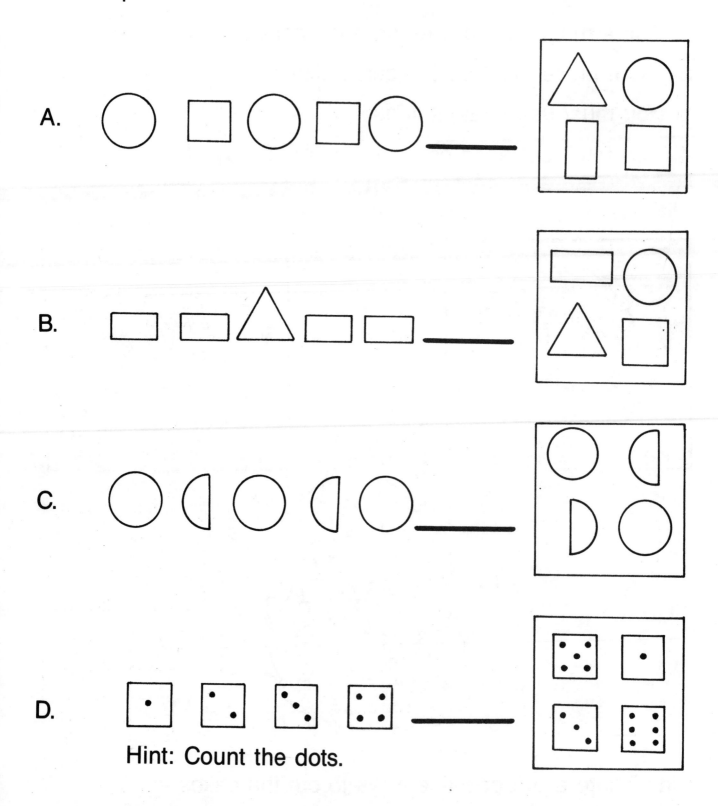

A.

B.

C.

D.

Hint: Count the dots.

Circle the shape that comes next.

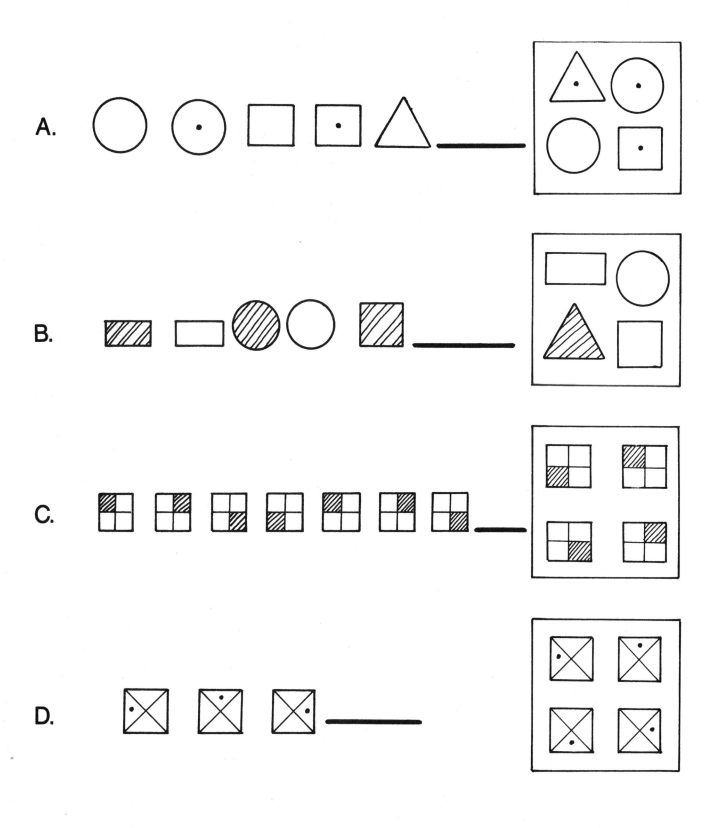

A.

B.

C.

D.

Circle the shape that comes next.

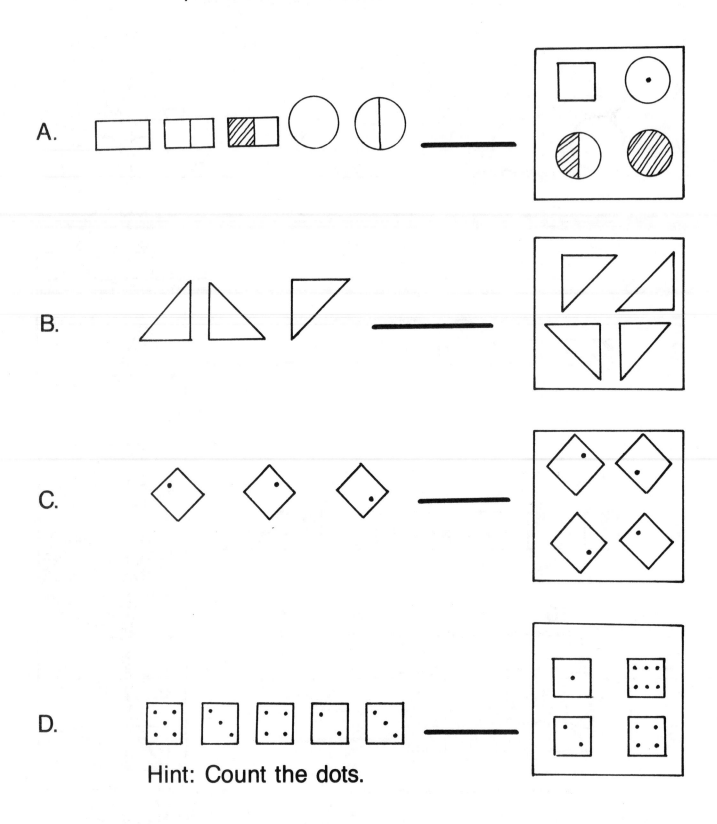

A.

B.

C.

D.

Hint: Count the dots.

Circle the missing number. Write it on the line.

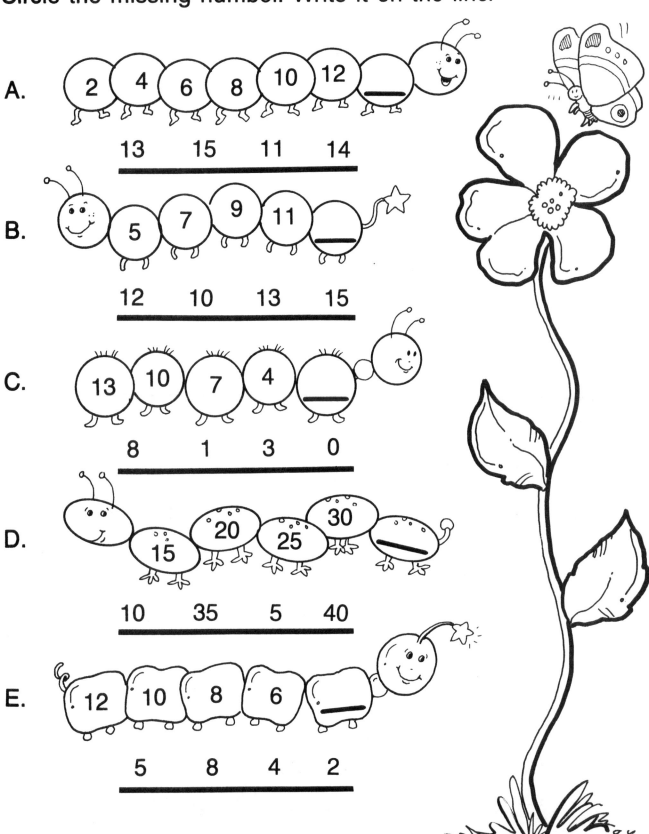

A. 2 4 6 8 10 12 ___

    13   15   11   14

B. 5 7 9 11 ___

    12   10   13   15

C. 13 10 7 4 ___

    8   1   3   0

D. 15 20 25 30 ___

    10   35   5   40

E. 12 10 8 6 ___

    5   8   4   2

Write the missing number on the line.

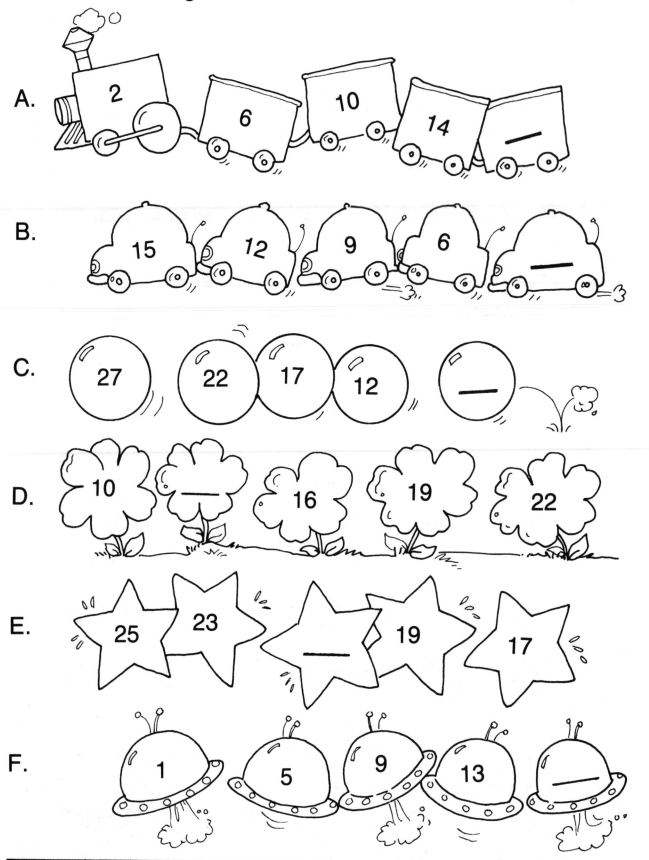

A. 2   6   10   14   ___

B. 15   12   9   6   ___

C. 27   22   17   12   ___

D. 10   ___   16   19   22

E. 25   23   ___   19   17

F. 1   5   9   13   ___

Write the missing numbers on the lines.

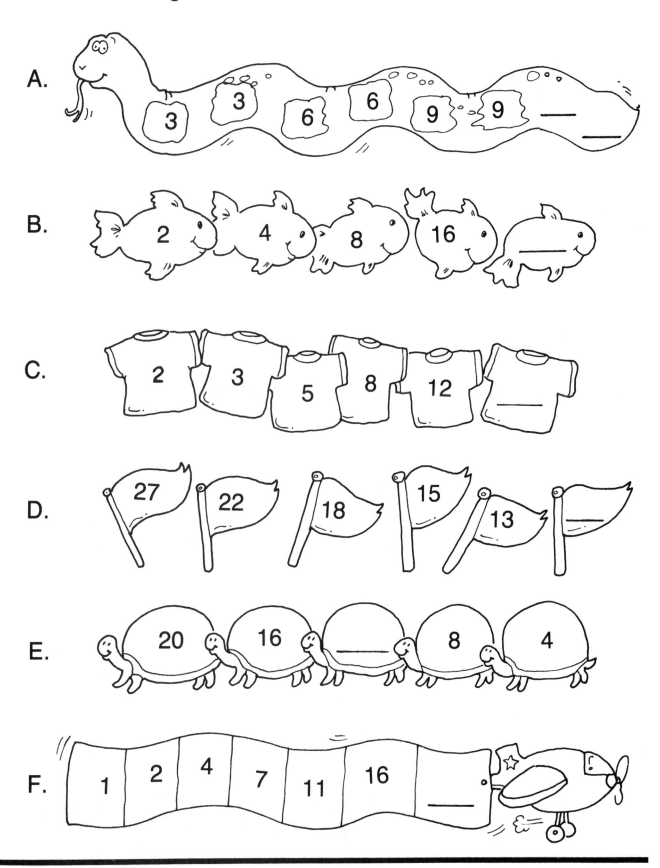

A. 3 3 6 6 9 9 ___

B. 2 4 8 16 ___

C. 2 3 5 8 12 ___

D. 27 22 18 15 13 ___

E. 20 16 ___ 8 4

F. 1 2 4 7 11 16 ___

Page 7:   6, 10, 11, 9, 8

Page 8:   6, 4, 8

Page 9:   11, 13, 21, 33, 19

Page 10:   18, 16, 14, 12, 10

Page 11:   75, 81, 99, 79, 87, 93

Page 12:   6, 12, 18, 24, 30

Pages 13, 14, 15: Answers will vary.

Page 16:   9

Page 17:   16

Page 18:   7, 2

Page 19:   7, 6, 2, 4

Page 20:   Answers will vary.

Page 21:   A. Jamal   B. Sarah   C. Eli   D. Matt   E. Rachel

Page 22:   A. Amanda   B. Kevin   C. Michele   D. Daniel

Page 23:   A. Teddy   B. Megan   C. Brittany   D. Tyrone

Page 24:   A. Timmy   B. Michael   C. Soraya   D. Tara   E. Nicky

Page 25:   A. Erin   B. Damon   C. Josh   D. Courtney   E. Sean

Page 26:   Hawks: 9 - 7 - 4   Eagles: 12 - 19 - 11

Page 27:   Top: 4; Middle: 7, 5; Bottom: 3, 6, 8

Page 28:   Top: 4; Middle: 6, 8; Bottom: 3, 5, 7

Page 29:   357, 375, 537, 573, 753, 735

Page 30:   168, 186, 681, 618, 861, 816   lowest score: 168   highest: 861

Page 31:

Dimes	Nickels	Pennies
1	1	0
1	0	5
0	1	10
0	2	5
0	0	15
0	3	0

Page 32:	Quarters	Dimes	Nickels
	2	0	0
	1	2	1
	1	1	3
	1	0	5
	0	0	10
	0	1	8
	0	2	6
	0	3	4
	0	4	2
	0	5	0

Page 33: 9 quarters, 7 nickels

Page 34: Ryan: 3, Breanna: 5, Alisha: 7

Page 35: Luis: 5, Henry: 9, Jimmy: 10

Page 36: Erica: 3, Hilary: 5, Morgan: 10

Page 37: Adam: 15, Josh: 7, Teddy: 9

Page 38: Answers will vary.

Page 39: 1) watercolors, crayons   2) markers, crayons   3) markers, crayons, paper

Page 40: 1) board game, puzzle   2) 2 board games   3) board game, book

Pages 41-42: 1) hamburger, fries, milk   2) apple, hot dog   3) 2 hot dogs, 1 milk   4) hot dog, hamburger, milk, french fries   5) $2.00   6) 2 hamburgers, fries, milk or 1 hamburger and 3 french fries   7) $10 bill   8) Answers will vary.

Page 43: Answers will vary.

Page 44: 6, 2, 2, or 4, 4, 2, or 3, 3, 4

Page 45: 7, 4, 4

Page 46: Possible answer: top - 4   middle - 5, 6   bottom - 3, 7, 2

Page 47: A. 10   B. 10   C. 10   D. 6   E. 8

Page 48: A. 3   B. 10   C. 12   D. 12   E. 8

Page 49: Answers will vary.

Page 50: 6 + 2 − 4

Page 51: 8 − 4 + 6 or 6 − 4 + 8

Page 52: 5 + 7 − 9 + 3 or 7 + 3 − 9 + 5

Page 53: Answers will vary.

Page 55: 14 squares

Page 56: 30 squares

Page 57: 8 triangles

Page 58: 11 rectangles

Page 59:
1. Clown — 10:00 A.M.
2. Magic — 10:30 A.M.
3. Dog — 11:30 A.M.

Page 60:
1. Seal — 10:30 A.M.
2. Elephant — 11:00 A.M.
3. Lunch — 12:00 P.M.
4. Monkey — 1:30 P.M.
5. Bird — 2:30 P.M.

Page 61:
1. Jack and the Beanstalk — 10:00 A.M.
2. Hansel and Gretel — 11:00 A.M.
3. Beauty and the Beast — 11:30 A.M.
4. Lunch — 12:30 P.M.
5. Red Riding Hood — 2:00 P.M.

Page 62: A = 4, B = 0, C = 2

Page 63: A = 3, B = 5, C = 1, D = 2, E = 4

Page 64: A = 4, B = 10, C = 2, D = 5, E = 6

Page 65:

$$1 - \underset{3}{\overset{2}{\textcircled{5}}} - 4$$

Pages 66-67:

```
      2                    2
3 — ①— 6        6 — ③ — 1
      7                    5

      3                    2
5 — ①— 4        1 — ⑤ — 4
      6                    3

      5                    3
2 — ①— 7        7 — ② — 1
      4                    5
```

Page 68:

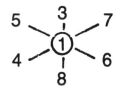

```
5   3   7        3   1   6
  ＼│／            ＼│／
4 —①— 6        2 —④— 5
  ／│＼            ／│＼
    8                7
```

Page 69:
```
8 — 1 — 6
|       |
4       2
|       |
3 — 5 — 7
```

Page 70: Answers will vary.
Page 71: Answers will vary: strawberry, cherry, tomato, etc.
Page 72: Answers will vary: skateboard, bike, wagon, etc.
Page 73: 1, 3, 5, 7, 9, 11, 13, 15, 17, 19
Page 74: 42, 44, 46, 48
Page 75: Answers will vary.

Page 76:
```
        Hilary
Stephen ◯ Valerie
        Casey
```

Page 77:
```
          Keith
    Max ◯ Courtney
         Sean
```

Page 78: Maple City
Page 79: Cherry Town; Hawthorne
Page 80: A. 12 cents   B. 21 cents   C. 30 cents

Page 81:

Zoonies	Roonies	Loonies
2	0	0
1	1	1
1	0	3
0	3	0
0	2	2
0	1	4
0	0	6

Page 82: A. 2 B. 4 C. 2

Page 83:

Dookles	Nanoops	Pogos
2	1	0
0	5	0
0	0	10
1	2	2
1	1	4
1	0	6
0	4	2
0	3	4
0	2	6
0	1	8
2	0	2

Page 84:

Page 85:

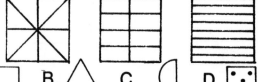

Page 86: A. □ B. △ C. ◖ D. ⚄

Page 87: A. △ B. □ C. ▨ D. ⊠

Page 88: A. ◑ B. ◺ C. ◇ D. ⊡

Page 89: A. 14 B. 13 C. 1 D. 35 E. 4
Page 90: A. 18 B. 3 C. 7 D. 13 E. 21 F. 17
Page 91: A. 12, 12 B. 32 C. 17 D. 12 E. 12 F. 22